Teachers: Have You Ever…?

Cheryl Kolker
Jan Landau

Published by Waldorf Publishing
2140 Hall Johnson Road
#102-345
Grapevine, Texas 76051
www.WaldorfPublishing.com

Teachers: Have You Ever...?

ISBN: 978-1-64316-611-7
Library of Congress Control Number: 2018943970

We dedicate our book to all the wonderful teachers, students, and parents who, over the years, made us laugh–whether they intended to or not.

Cheryl & Jan

Acknowledgments

Cheryl: To my wonderful family, who is the foundation of my life.

Jan: To my husband, Sam, who, for over 30 years, listened to all of my own experiences in the classroom and from day one said, "You should write a book!"

List of Contributors
Cheryl Kolker and Jan Landau

Marilyn Bleznak
Jan Capon
Jill Chapin
Kelly Cox
Beverly Davis
Bernie Goldstein
Liz Goldstein
Barbara Gordon
Judi Gottschalk
Sharon Gruby
Roxanne Hersh
Arlene Keeyes
Kelley King
Sam Landau
Carol Lazarus
Irene Lerner
Susan Liebman
Ellen Mann
Fran Miller
Jeri Moskowitz
Shelly Moses
Sonia Fox Ohlbaum
Marna Weiss Padowitz
Sheryl Rabinowitz
Vivian Rich
Naomi Shakhman
Dianne Shapp
Ellen Statman
Ellen Steindorf
Richard Strausz

Introduction

The purpose of *Teachers: Have You Ever...?* is to serve as an outlet for anyone who is presently working with, has ever worked with, or is contemplating working with children of all ages–fellow teachers, teacher assistants, administrators, and school employees–to be entertained, to laugh, to commiserate, and to identify and connect with our unique perspective as educators. It will also allow parents, grandparents, and relatives and friends of students who are presently in school, who have ever attended school, or who will attend school in the future, to gain a unique perspective, mostly through humor, of the challenges teachers experience every day and what they are really thinking during parent/teacher encounters.

Teachers: Have You Ever...?

1. Deliberately kicked a fellow teacher in the shin and heard her scream out in pain during a conference with an adamant "My Child Never Does Anything Wrong!" parent?

2. Screamed out in pain when kicked by your co-teacher during a parent/teacher conference?

3. Accidentally thrown out a book report and told the child you never got it?

4. Clipped a kid's throat when helping him zip up his jacket?

5. Dropped food on the floor at a class program, put it back on the plate and served it to parents?

6. Made a child stand on his broken leg all afternoon? A boy came in whimpering about hurting his leg at recess. I looked . . . blood, no bruises, no swelling. "You'll be fine. You can be my helper this afternoon." He helped me pass out and collect papers, hand out supplies, etc. The next day he came to school with a cast on his leg.

7. Spilled paint on a child's 11x14 glossy portrait brought to class by his grandparents to share on Grandparents Day?

8. Asked a parent when she was due–and she wasn't pregnant?

9. Been informally approached by a parent to discuss her child, and you can't remember who her child is?

10. Gone to work wearing your new singing Valentine's Day underwear and have it accidentally play music while you were giving the kids a spelling test?

11. In tears, brought your dead dog to school in the back of your car to leave lesson plans for the sub because the vet to whom you were bringing the dog's body didn't open until 9:00?

12. Put a nasty note on the window of another teacher's car because she constantly took up two parking spaces? In the teacher's lounge the next day, you burst out laughing when a teacher complained, "Some bitch put a note on my car about my parking."

13. Had to convince a co-teacher to remove her homemade tip jar from her desk even though she is adamant that she works harder than a Starbucks' barista?

14. Avoided a co-worker who always seemed ready to pounce on you like a cat whenever you walked by her classroom, grabbed your arm, pulled you into her room and made you feel like a hostage until you gushingly admired *her* creativity and projects over and over again?

15. Rolled your eyes to fellow teachers at a mother who picked up her child from school as scantily clad as a Playboy Bunny? You didn't realize that her husband had seen you until he winked and gave you an "okay" sign as

he got back in his car.

16. Avoided a parent...just to avoid that parent?

17. Received a gift bag from a child with nothing in it and wondered what you should write in a thank-you note?

18. Sat at your desk with your legs tightly crossed wishing that there was a Dedicated Depends for Teachers who never have a chance to take a bathroom break during the day?

19. Snuck a piece of chocolate in your mouth during class when you thought the kids were not looking and be caught in the act when little Sari called out, "Hey! That's not fair! You always tell us that unless we have enough for everyone, we can't eat in class"?

20. Called your principal a "demeaning, delusional, repulsive, repugnant, compulsive liar" (rich with expletives) to his face and still kept your job?

21. Accidentally passed gas, looked all around the classroom, and made the statement: "Someone needs to go to the restroom!"?

22. Had a meeting with a second grader and his parents to discuss starting a daily behavior chart both at school and at home, only to be told by the father, "That ain't gonna work! I don't believe in them behavior charts. I'm gonna take away something that really counts. We got ourselves a Volkswagen and a Cadillac. Michael, you

hear me good. You ain't gonna drive the Volkswagen no more!'"?

23. After a particularly rough and tough parent/teacher conference week, secretly wished that you taught at a school for orphans?

24. Had a kid ask to go to the bathroom and, when he returned, whisper in your ear, "I have a problem. On my way to the bathroom I had to fart, but the fart part didn't work, and now I need to change my clothes"?

25. Had to tell a parent that she must teach her fourth-grade child to wipe his own ass?

26. Had a former fifth-grade student about to graduate high school, come back to visit you, climb on top of your desk, and lift up a ceiling tile to look for his secret stash of candy? Lo and behold, the candy was still there, and Liam enjoyed every stale bite.

27. Stopped for dinner at an Italian restaurant while on an annual fourth-grade overnight trip? As my colleagues and I were trying to get the kids and attending adults organized, several parent chaperones stood up, smiled, and nonchalantly waved goodbye as they walked out the door.
Their explanation when I caught up with them and asked where they were going...they don't eat carbs and were going to a nearby restaurant for sushi and a cocktail. But not to worry, they assured me, other chaperones were kind enough to watch their groups for them.

28. Had a kindergarten student tell you in a very complimentary manner that your gray rain jacket is a perfect match for the hair on the very top of your head? In fact, she added, sometimes her grandmother has the same color hair that I do, but she goes to a magic store that makes the gray disappear. I couldn't wait to get the address of the same magic store.

29. Had a child make you feel very old? When I brought my record player to class to show the kids how I listened to music when I was their age and held up a record from my collection, Levi called out, "Wow! What a giant CD! That must have enough songs on it to play for a week!"

30. Received an 8"x10" digital photo frame loaded with at least 100 pictures of your student and his family for you and your family to enjoy during the holidays?

31. Sent a disrespectful third grade student to the school office to speak with the school-counselor for the umpteenth time? As per the agreed-upon procedure following numerous parent/teacher meetings, the child called his father to self-report his unacceptable behavior. After listening to his father's loud and angry reprimands over the phone, the child screamed into the receiver, "Go have a wet dream!", slammed down the phone, and stormed out of the room.

32. Upon her son's suspension seven years later, have the same parent acknowledge that she knew her son brought a vibrator to school on Valentine's Day as a gag gift and very dismissively reply, "I told him he'd

get caught!'"?

33. Excitedly been offered a candy bar from your first grade student? When the proud seven-year old pulled a half-wrapped chocolate bar out of her grimy, sweaty sock in eager anticipation of sharing it with you, you realized that you not only had to graciously accept it but take a bite as well.

34. Asked students in your kindergarten class to bring in examples of objects shaped like the letter "O" for the monthly show-and-tell for parents, only to have a parent gasp when she realized that the letter "O" her daughter shared was actually the rim of the diaphragm she had thrown in the bathroom trash the night before, after she discovered that her very naughty dog had chewed up the entire center part?

35. Had a child give you a beautiful bottle of "*Eau de Toilette*" with an embarrassed explanation: "My mom said that this bottle of toilet water is for you, but if I were you I wouldn't use it"?

36. Taught your own child and, because of his continuous rude behavior, had to call your husband to school for a mandatory parent/teacher meeting?

37. Had a student tell you that her research assignment was stolen by the Russian Mafia and have it emphatically confirmed by her mother?

38. Had a kindergarten student proudly tell you that it was *her* pee that was given to the school nurse instead

of that of the student who had to provide several urine samples a day for a diabetes check?

39. After making suggestions to a parent about how she could best help her child at home to improve his reading level, been told in a very condescending tone, "You care too much about my child's education"?

40. Would you rather pick up dog poop at a park or have to think of positive comments to write on the report cards of students who have given you hell all year?

41. Cried the night before returning to your classroom after summer vacation, winter break, spring break and, let's face it, every Sunday night?

42. Had a conference about a student with his mother and her non-credentialed, tag-along, life-coach/friend who spoke for the clueless parent and gave *you* tips about how to teach?

43. Wished you could set up a fortune telling booth at your school's Halloween carnival to warn certain parents that they need therapy immediately so that their children do not end up in prison someday?

44. Been asked by a student if you could suggest a book about the "veal" because that was the animal about which she chose to do a report?

45. Asked a student to research the clothes people wore during Colonial times? Five minutes later, the child shouted to you from across the room, "Mrs. L., I don't

think I should be on this site," and held up his tablet with a picture of a woman wearing black lace stockings and nothing else?

46. Had to frustratingly rearrange the desks in your classroom a million times because there were no ideal configurations that would keep a number of extremely difficult students from sitting next to each other?

47. Had a student turn multiple shades of green while standing in front of your desk and not had your wastebasket in the immediate proximity?

48. Had a highly disruptive student refuse to go to the office to be disciplined by the principal and have 27 other kids' eyes bug out of their heads in anticipation of you strangling him?

49. Had to explain to your students that what you just yelled out was not what they heard after you had stapled your finger to a set of papers?

50. Accompanied the child who had given you a bag of your favorite dark chocolate kisses earlier that day to the   principal's office? It seems that when Ethan mistakenly thought no one was looking, he took the bag of candy out of your not-so-secret candy drawer and stuffed it in the   desk of a student he wanted to get in trouble because they had a fight during recess. I was truly dumbfounded at the principal's clueless response to the significance of   the office visit. "Well, you know, Mrs. K.," he said in front of the student, "the candy wasn't really yours in the first place."

51. Had a child wet his pants and the floor beneath his seat, walk up to you, and whisper in your ear, "I don't know who made the floor wet, but it wasn't me"?

52. Had a parent tell you not to be concerned with his son's poor aptitude and attitude for math because Aaron is assured a job in the family business–just not in the finance department?

53. Had a parent forget to pack her child's lunch and become very annoyed when you asked her to bring her daughter's lunch to school before noon? (After all, the mom did not want to miss her manicure appointment.) Her "directive" was to have other children and/or me share our lunches with her daughter with a very specific list of do's and don'ts: no white bread, no processed meats, no cheddar cheese, no crunchy peanut butter, strawberry jelly only, a sliced red apple (yes, it had to be sliced), and chips with as little salt as possible.

54. Had a preschooler come to school every day dressed like a hooker in bright fuchsia lipstick, purple eyeshadow, mini-sized high heels, and short shorts?

55. After teaching basic genetics to a third-grade class, had a student shout in disbelief: "That doesn't make sense. How could I have on my father's 'jeans' when I was in my mother's belly?"

56. Had a first-grade child bring her mother's *very* valuable emerald earrings, diamond ring, and diamond bracelet to school to give to some of her classmates as

gifts? Naomi's "generosity" was only discovered when, while tucking their daughter in bed that night, the parents of one of the "recipients" of the gifts noticed the sparkling diamond tennis bracelet dangling from their daughter's wrist.

57. Had a child select the historical fiction book *Shades of Gray* by Carolyn Reeder in the school library and yell out in shock: "Mrs. G., this is the book my mom didn't want me to know about because it's all about sex"? I assured Lizzie that the book she chose was not the same book her mother's book group was reading, and that *Shades of Gray* is definitely appropriate for her study of the Civil War. At the end of the day, I sent an email to her mom telling her about our library experience and suggested that she keep her copy of *Fifty Shades of Grey* by E. L. James under lock and key.

58. Had a second grader knowingly, mischievously, and laughingly sing his original composition of "I Love My Penis" in front of his shocked classmates?

59. Had a Russian parent advise you that when her son exhibits oppositional defiant behavior, to just take him aside and harshly whisper in his ear, "Siberia, Siberia, Siberia"?

60. Had a parent report you to the principal of a very prestigious Catholic school because her extremely quiet and shy daughter, Mary Christina, was not given the role of Mary in the all-school Christmas show? One of the reasons her daughter was given the name Mary Christina, the distraught mother cried, was to ensure her

a starring role in the Christmas show every year.

61. Literally and unintentionally drooled over the shoulder of a child who was eating a delicious plate of sushi because you had not eaten breakfast, and all you had for lunch was a granola bar?

62. Received a year-end gift from a very wealthy parent and recognized it as the same freebie you had been given the week before at the cosmetics counter at Nordstrom?

63. Had a student burst out crying because you wouldn't let her share her very favorite book, *Go the Fuck to Sleep,* by Adam Mansbach, with the class?

64. Had a student accidentally call you "Grandma" the day after you were told by your doctor that you were officially in menopause?

65. Tried to improve the taste of the undrinkable coffee from the teachers' lounge by adding four packets of sugar and six mini dark chocolate bars to your mug? A few minutes later, you had to ask a student to run and get the school nurse because you thought your heart was going to beat out of your chest.

66. Had a parent ask you to watch her two-year-old child during your break so that she could go food shopping-for just a few items, of course?

67. Given your school secretary a sticky note with the words attached to a homework sheet: "Please make

three copies" and have her make three copies of the sticky note request instead of copies of the homework sheet?

68. Had a child psychiatrist call you before school to ask you to talk to his sick child on the phone in order for her to accept the fact that she couldn't come to school with a fever?

69. Sent weekly emails and photos to parents about on-going class activities and then be told by a parent, who you know received the emails, that he would like better communication about what is going on in class?

70. Received a beautiful, cellophane wrapped imitation red rose for Valentine's Day from a very modest fifth-grade student? And when the rose was unwrapped, the petals unfolded to reveal a pair of lacy, red thong underwear.

71. Been a young, and understandably nervous male teacher at your very first parent/teacher conference and have a mother whip out her breast—literally bare-breasted—and begin to nurse her six-week-old infant while continuing the dialogue?

72. Been given a lovely bottle of red wine and a pill bottle labeled 'Prozac' by a group of sixth-grade parents on the first day of school?

73. Been seriously asked by a parent about her son, "Will you love Quinn as much as I do?" at Back to School Night?

74. Dealt with parents who are needy, controlling, competitive, demanding, disrespectful, enabling and enabled, hovering, and those who only see their children through rose-colored, Lasik surgeried eyes?

75. Had a high school student, who is a tenor, suddenly sing alto because he was masturbating during choir?

76. Had a fourth-grade parent show you a jelly jar filled with the nail clippings of her daughter that she had saved from the time her daughter was born? What the mom loved most about this collection were the rainbow-colored nail polish clippings that reflected her daughter's colorful personality.

77. Had a parent bring a hemorrhoid pillow to school for her first-grade son because the chairs were too hard for his sensitive butt cheeks?

78. Had a parent scream at you, "I'm going to f ** king kill you," after you politely, but firmly, informed her, through her car window at pick-up time, that she may no longer keep the teacher on duty waiting an extra 20 minutes every day while she parked her car at a distance and made phone calls?

79. Had parents insist that their third-grade son could read and comprehend an adult level biography about Albert Einstein for his book report? After all, they said, I told them at the last teacher conference that I was delighted that their son, who was just about reading at

grade level at the beginning of the school year, was now assessed to be reading above grade level.

80. Had a second-grade parent list on his child's home reading log *Money Magazine* because he believed that it is never too early to prepare his son for the family business?

81. Had a culminating at-home project about the California Missions become a parent-made project competition rather than just a presentation of the children's own work and creativity?

82. Had a child bring his mom's credit card to school to pay for a book from a book club that cost $1.99, along with a request for a receipt?

83. Had to sit through two hours of your school's erroneously titled Talent Show not only once during school hours, but also at two mandatory teachers' attendance performances at night?

84. Given an assignment to your first graders to interview a worker in their community for Career Day and then be asked by a student's mother if *you* would accompany her daughter to the interview? "Why?" you hesitantly asked. The parent had no trouble telling you that she and her husband were going to be in Europe weeks before the assignment was due, and she wanted to be sure Sophie was able to complete her work on time.

85. Had to notify the principal of the school that you were very concerned because one of the chaperones and

her carpool with five students was late in returning to school from a class trip to the Science Museum? When the parent was contacted on her cell phone, she apologized for her tardiness and explained that she was waiting for the kids to finish their lunch at a local fast-food restaurant. Although she meekly acknowledged signing a form that clearly stated that chaperones were not permitted to make food purchases while at the museum, she did not think the same rule applied once they left the museum.

86. Pretended not to notice that your principal fell asleep while observing your lesson? At the follow-up meeting a few hours later, the principal complimented you on your model lesson.

87. Unintentionally modeled the perfect lesson? At a celebratory pizza party for the class, which happened to follow a lesson about idioms, I began choking on a piece of pizza. As my eyes watered and my face turned red, most of the kids were quite concerned. One student started pounding on my back while others came running to me with bottles of water. While still trying to get my choking under control, I knew that my lesson on idioms was successful when eight-year-old Addison pointed at me and blurted out to the class, "She's not really choking, so don't worry. She's just showing us what it means when you bite off more than you can chew!"

88. Had a very supportive parent so completely exasperated with her son's ongoing challenging and disruptive behavior, that as she was leaving the principal's office after yet another emotionally exhausting team

meeting with the teachers, principal, and school counselor, announce with a wry smile and mock sincerity, "At this point, I hope you know that if Noah was kidnapped I wouldn't pay the ransom"? She then handed each person in attendance a very generous gift card with a note that read: *This is the least I can do to thank you for going above and beyond for my son. By the way, there's much more to come for the first one to volunteer to have him live with you for the rest of the school year.*

89. Had a very precocious five-year-old, while on a "time-out" in the school office for biting another child, try to call 911 on one of the secretary's phones because in his words, "That's what my mommy and daddy told me to do if I'm in trouble"?

90. Had a child bring a pregnancy test strip to school when it was her day to share and announce to the class, "I'm going to be a big sister"?

91. Offered a perpetually unhappy parent at your private school the phone number for the public school down the street?

92. Hopped behind the wheel of a parent's illegally parked vehicle that was holding up traffic at dismissal—keys were left in—driven it to a designated parking spot, and watched with smug satisfaction the perplexed look on the parent's face when he came back to where he thought he parked his car and couldn't find it?

93. Been told by a young colleague that when she was trying to settle down her tenth-grade science class,

she must have shouted out in exasperation, "There is no room for foreplay in the lab!"? Some of the kids burst out laughing, and one kid called out, "Mrs. W., I think you meant *horseplay*."

94. Along with two other teachers, spent hours preparing two weeks of classwork for three siblings who would be missing school because of the family's annual trip to Australia? When the family returned, the parent sent emails to each of the teachers requesting that we use our lunch breaks to help her children complete all of the classwork they didn't have time to work on during their vacation.

95. Had a parent ask you to keep your class work for all students at a minimum because her child would be missing school for a two-day birthday celebration at Disneyland?

96. Watched in amazement as a high school senior tried to stuff his basketball into his locker thinking that if he turned it around and around multiple times, it would be able to fit?

97. Discussed the importance of a strategic plan when working with a group of fifth graders on creating a business for their semester project? Jordan, one of the students, raised his hand and said that his parents had a strategic plan for him to be successful in life by only allowing him to have playdates with kids who are positive influences. Ken, a member of the group who was always getting in trouble, yelled, "That leaves me out!"

98. Caught a parent of a kindergartner leaving your classroom just as you arrived and very matter-of-factly inform you that she had just changed her daughter's seat because she—the parent—was upset that her daughter was not sitting next to her best friend?

99. Had a student misspell the four-letter swear word that she carved into your classroom cupboard door? Your first reaction was that she obviously had not yet processed the phonics lesson you recently taught about the short "u" sound.

100. At the dedication of a beautiful garden on our campus in memory of a beloved teacher who had recently died, overheard one child tell her friend, "This is where all the teachers will get buried when they die"?

101. Had to tactfully suggest to a fourth-grade parent volunteer that she dress more modestly when she volunteers in the future because her size DD, silicone-filled implants, barely concealed beneath a shirt that was at least two sizes too small, were somewhat of a class distraction?

102. Worked at a very small private school located in a house? While presenting a lesson to your students, you just happened to look out your classroom window and saw a masseuse giving a naked woman a massage in the house next door?

103. Sat at the front of your classroom while the children were sitting on the floor in front of you, twirled your foot, and have one of your shoes fly off and hit a

very shocked six-year-old in the face?

104. Had a parent come to your classroom after school once a week with her housekeeper whose job must have obviously included cleaning the daughter's schoolroom desk?

105. Had a parent insist to your school principal that the carpet in your kindergarten room must be ripped out because her child was allergic to dust?

106. Had a pajama clad first-grade student show up to your class 15 minutes late carrying his clothes in a brown paper bag, and hear his exasperated mom exclaim, "You deal with him!" and walk out of the room?

107. Taken fourth-grade students on an airplane trip to Sacramento, California's state capital, and have one of them comment, "I've never flown economy before"?

108. Been asked by a fellow teacher to borrow some twine because she wanted to tie an overly active student to his desk?

109. Had a first grader ask you if you have sex with your husband?

110. Had a first grader tell you that her mom said her dad has to sleep in the guest bedroom in their house until he loses 20 pounds?

111. Had an extremely pudgy father come in for a serious discussion about his child and, as he stood in

front of your desk in a partially unbuttoned, coffee splat-
tered, food-stained shirt, you had to concentrate as hard
as you could on not looking at his outie belly button that
seemed to be staring you right in the face?

112. Had a parent allow her hyperactive son to come
to school dressed as Edward Scissorhands on Halloween, complete with pointed scissors glued to his gloves?

113. Had a kindergarten student bring a tool box
with a real saw for Show and Tell and not understand
why you would not allow him to pass it around in class?

114. In the middle of an assembly at which most of
the audience was seated on the floor, had to embarrass-
ingly offer a parent a chair because the fourth and fifth
graders sitting behind her were elbowing each other and
laughing hysterically at her exposed butt crack, thong
underwear, and heart-shaped tattoo?

115. When discussing the 2016 presidential election, had a child ask if you thought you would still be
alive at the 2020 election?

116. Had a fourth-grade student ask how old you are
and be told, "You don't look 54, and I don't mean that as
a compliment"?

117. Had your second-grade students ask you to
look up information about the author of a book you were
reading to them? When one of the students figured out
that the author died when he was 50 years old, another
student shouted out, "Wow! He died of old age!"

118. Had a first-grade student ask if you had any kids? When you replied that you had a 23-year-old son and a 19-year-old daughter, she then asked, "Well, how old are you?" When you jokingly responded, "I'm nineteen years old," she replied, "Are you and your daughter twins?"

119. Had a parent ask the principal if her fifth-grade daughter could bring her newly adopted kitten to class for emotional support during an assessment for sixth-grade math placement?

120. Had fellow teachers complain ad nauseam about parents not reading and responding to emails, and then have the same teachers not read or correctly respond to a time-sensitive email that you sent to them?

121. Been afraid that you might lose impulse control and say what you were really thinking to a parent who loudly admonished you in front of his child? He was furious that you would not allow his daughter to retake a math test a second time after she earned, in the parent's words, "a disappointing B" on the first retest?

122. Caught a parent chaperone smoking pot in the hotel bathroom on an overnight class trip?

123. Smelled anything worse than a fifth-grade classroom after the kids come back from lunch/recess followed by PE on a very hot day in May?

124. Had your principal tell you that you could be

replaced by an eight-dollar-an-hour employee if you don't run an after-school program?

125. Put an "X" on the communal jar of pretzels in the teachers' room as a warning to other teachers that this jar was for the exclusive use of the male principal who we were sure never washed his hands after he flushed?

126. Had a child bring 100 crisp new five-dollar bills to class to celebrate the first 100 days of school?

127. Felt like responding to a group of parents who asked why you are retiring early: "Just look in the mirror!"?

128. Secretly wished that there was a Valium laced salt lick in the teachers' lounge with the sign: "Use As Needed"?

129. Had a kindergarten student ask you if he could go the bathroom and when you replied, "Yes," look at you and burst out in tears? When you asked him, "What's the matter?" he cried, "I don't know how to wipe!"

130. In order to prevent a potential parent uprising, had to report a fellow teacher because of her solution to what she considered an unfair request from the principal that children not be allowed to leave the classroom during standardized testing? Instead of taking the kids to the bathroom before the test, she set up a partition in the back of her classroom behind which were several wastebaskets lined with garbage bags for kids who couldn't hold it.

131. Been accused of being a member of the KKK because you wore an all-white tent dress to school?

132. Had Kelsey, your new puppy, chew to shreds the homework assignment completed by one of your students, whose name also happened to be Kelsey? The next day I had to sheepishly admit to two-legged Kelsey (with photos for proof) that my naughty pup really and truly did eat her homework.

133. Had to politely decline the request of the grand-mother of one of your students when she asked you to please speak to her daughter-in-law about her permissive parenting skills at the upcoming parent/teacher conference?

134. After a first-grade girl shared the news that the tooth fairy left three dollars under her pillow, had to deal with an avalanche of student tears and parent emails when her classmate very emphatically made the double pronouncement: "My sister told me that the Tooth Fairy and Santa Claus are really fake"?

135. Received an email from a parent that read: *With the new and ongoing awareness of sexual harassment, are the kids still allowed to play two-touch football?*

136. When teaching a social studies lesson, asked the kids to bring in objects that miners might have bartered with during the California Gold Rush instead of using money? Among the items brought to class were beads, coins, shells, bottle caps, buttons, and pieces of

colorful yarn. Jake was very excited to show everyone a canvas bag filled with what seemed to be very old tin stars and said, "You know how sometimes people say bucks instead of money? My grandmother told me that these stars originally belonged to my great-great grandfather's grandfather and that the first Starbucks started when miners used them during the gold rush to buy coffee."

137. Had a student gently shake you awake after you fell asleep while working with a first-grade reading group following three sleepless nights with your four-month-old twins?

139. Had a parent accuse you of stealing her child's lunch money? The next day she sent you an email apology saying that she found the lunch money envelope at the bottom of her purse.

140. Had to ask a student teacher to change his sweatshirt on school spirit day because the school colors he was proudly wearing depicted a large, overflowing beer can?

141. Had a student double-talk so creatively and animatedly that you actually began to believe that what you knew was the correct answer might be wrong?

142. Had a team meeting with a parent about confidence building strategies for her extremely shy, quiet, and timid child? Being a former teacher herself, she nailed my description of her daughter's behavior by saying, "So, in other words, Bea is so quiet in class that

you wish you had a stethoscope to check if she has a heartbeat."

143. After experiencing an excessively high number of children in each class with major behavioral needs, wondered if the criteria for admission to the small private school at which you taught was based on three things: having two pencils, a package of writing paper, and a pulse?

144. After a student researched the similarities and coincidences between Abraham Lincoln and John Fitzgerald Kennedy, have him include in his report what he was obviously not meant to overhear his father say: "In 1862, Lincoln was in Monroe, Maryland, and in 1962 Kennedy was in Marilyn Monroe"?

145. Around election time, had your students discuss the attributes of a good president and have all but one child agree that a president should be involved in world affairs. When asked why she didn't think that was an important concern for a president, he replied, "Why should a president have to go to everyone's weddings and Bar Mitzvahs?"

146. Had a seventh-grade public school student ask if you are Jewish because you were out of school the first two days of the Jewish holiday of Passover? When you replied, "Yes," he said, "You don't look like you just came out of the desert."

147. Had the frustrated parent of a student, who was a bellyache-complaining, frequent flyer to the school

nurse, walk into the nurse's office with a year's supply of crackers and the following note:

There's nothing wrong with my daughter, I know.
I could feel your frustration with Lisa grow,
Please don't call me when to your office again she goes,
JUST GIVE HER A F *** *ING CRACKER!*

148. Had a parent chaperone keep the kids entertained on a field trip by playing charades and pantomiming the word 'proctologist'?

149. On a field trip to the zoo, had the docent explain to the second-grade class that an animal who sleeps during the day and is awake at night is nocturnal, and an animal who is awake during the day and sleeps at night is diurnal? Eight-year-old Jason eagerly raised his hand to ask the question, "My parents sleep in the nude. What do you call them?"

150. On an overnight class trip, had a parent chaperone with misguided delusions of noblesse oblige upgrade his accommodations and that of his two charges
—his twin sons—to a suite with unlimited room service?

151. Been horror-struck when you realized that you pressed "reply" instead of "forward" in response to an email that you intended to share with your principal from a very difficult parent with your added comment: *This is a nice email from Merle K. for a change. She must be on meds!*"? Parent response? "You're right, and they're working!"-- xxx Merle xxx

152. As a teacher in a Los Angeles school, received a beautifully wrapped gift and note from your student on Teacher Appreciation Day? When you unwrapped the gift, there was a book with the following stamp on the cover: "Please return to the Skokie, Illinois, Public Library."

153. Opened a beautifully wrapped book and lovely note handed to you by a very excited and eager-to-please student and tried to stifle a laugh when you realized that this gift was most definitely not meant for you? The note, written from the child's parent to a young woman who had just started her career, read: *Judi, congratulations on landing such a great first job. The sky's the limit. I wish I had been given a book like this when I graduated college.* The title of the just unwrapped book: *How to Succeed in Business Without a Penis: Secrets and Strategies for the Working Woman* by Karen Salmansohn. Fifteen minutes later, the student's mother sent me the following frantic email: *SOS! I hope it's not too late to tell you not to let any of the kids see the gift that Michelle gave you. I just realized she must have accidentally grabbed the gift bag that was for my friend's daughter.*

154. As the school counselor, had to suspend a student for his ongoing disrespectful and disobedient behavior? When the child's mother came to school to pick up her son, she looked at me with daggers in her eyes and, while hugging and consoling her child, very loudly said to him, "Sammy, let's get a sundae and go to a movie."

155. At Back-to-School Night, had a father of a third grader ask for a written outline of your objectives, goals, and curriculum for the entire year because he wanted to make sure his daughter will be prepared for the rigors of an Ivy League university?

156. Mistakenly marked one of your most rambunctious student absent when he entered the room and took his seat without causing a scene for the first time all year?

157. Motivated an entire fifth-grade class to read a novel about the Puritans in Colonial America by accidentally introducing it as one of your favorite books, *The Bitch of Blackbird Pond*? I only realized my gaffe when one of the boys held up his book, *The Witch of Blackbird Pond,* and said with a knowing smirk, "Well, Mrs. L, I guess the rest of us are reading the sequel."

158. Walked behind a group of fifth-grade boys who were headed to the bathroom to discuss the "highlights" of the puberty movie they had just watched in class? When I asked the not-so-newly enlightened young men why they were bringing rulers into the bathroom, Josh, the youngest of four brothers, informed me, "My brothers gave me a heads-up on what the movie is about. They said that what the movie left out was that our 'things' should be seven inches long."

159. On a daily basis, had to deal with an unreasonably demanding, interfering, insecure parent of a child in your class who just happened to be the teacher in the classroom next to yours?

160. On the first day of school, told a second-grade student that you had the pleasure of teaching her mother when she was in second grade at the same school. As Mitzi nodded her head with a huge smile, another student called out, "That can't be true. If you were Mitzi's mother's teacher, you'd be dead by now."

161. Received an email from a third-grade mom who wanted to know why Maxi, her daughter, had to bring eight quarters to school that day? I certainly had no idea. However, the answer became very clear when all of the girls walked into the classroom after recess holding their very own Maxi Pad. It seems that when Maxi saw the Maxi Pad dispenser in the bathroom, she thought it would be fun to give each of her friends a gift that would always remind them of her.

162. Five weeks into the new school year, called a meeting with the mother of a new child in the school to discuss your concerns about her daughter's difficulty comprehending basic math and science concepts? Both the science teacher and I were confused because at the beginning of the school year the mother made it a point to tell both of us that her daughter has "superior intelligence and is a potential Mensa candidate." Seemingly not at all surprised or concerned about her daughter's lack of progress, the mother grabbed each of our hands, squeezed them tightly, looked directly into our eyes, and said, "Don't worry. You'll see. Just like flowers, Lola will bloom in the spring."

163. Had a parent walk her red-eyed, slimy green runny-nosed four-year-old daughter into your classroom

and tell you how much Ridley is looking forward to your field trip to the zoo? When I warily asked the mom if she had checked her daughter's temperature before coming to school, the parent became indignant and admonished me for asking such a rude question. Sure enough, as soon as we got to the zoo, Ridley laid down on the ground and tearfully asked if she could take a nap. To make matters worse, her mother did not answer her cell phone or return the two messages I left. As a result, I had to carry Ridley all around the zoo. Three days later I had to stay home from work with a temperature and a raging cold.

164. Worked in your room during a prep and be startled by a sound coming from the vicinity of your open window? When you looked over, you saw first one foot attached to a leg and then another come through the window and land on the counter next to your sink. The rest of an unknown woman's body appeared. A parent, not even one of yours, apologized and explained that she was late for her Guest Reader appointment in another class, and thought this route would be quicker than the required front door office sign-in route!

165. Had a parent tell you that if her child spends three to five minutes doing a worksheet that is below his zone of proximal development, he will become lazy and never develop stamina or fortitude to accomplish higher things in life?

166. Had a parent tell you not to contact him or his wife regarding any problems with their child because they are extremely busy people? I was told I should only contact the *au pair*!

167. Had to tell a parent, who was also a teacher at your school, that it was very disruptive when she interrupted the class to deliver a frappuccino to her daughter during math instruction?

168. Had a parent tell you that she was very worried that her fourth-grade daughter was not "intellectually curious" because she did not want to watch PBS specials about the Amish and global warming?

169. Had better control of your class when you spoke to them in a made-up language than when you spoke to them in English?

170. As an April Fool's joke, told your students that your identical twin sister from England would be subbing for you the next day and to be sure to be on their very best behavior? The next day, after two hours of the charade and maintaining a British accent, two of the kids told you that you were a lot nicer and prettier than your sister.

171. After discussing the importance of being your best self-advocate and questioning what you do not understand, played a trick on your tenth-grade advanced-math group on April Fools' Day by writing a crazy, nonsensical, very long and complicated math problem on the board? When no one in the group could successfully solve the problem after fifteen minutes, you showed them the completely made up "correct" answer. "Any questions?" None! The next day, Matt, a student whose mother was a college math professor, told you

that his mom looked at the problem and agreed with your answer.

172. Asked a student why he had a water balloon in his desk and have him respond, "Never mind, Mr. Bernard, you're not going to find any of my answers acceptable, so I'll just get rid of it."

173. Entered your room after spring break and smelled something foul? After looking all around for a dead rodent, you find two moldy tuna sandwiches, at least a month old, in a student's desk?

174. Busted a parent for completing her son Eli's homework in his Google docs? It was a dead give-away when the child came to school the next day and was very upfront in telling you that he didn't finish his homework because he didn't feel well and fell asleep at 6:30 p.m.?

175. Incredulously stared at your principal when he called an unscheduled staff meeting the day before the new school year began to say that the daily schedule had been changed? What remained loudly unsaid was that the schedule had been changed to accommodate the needs of two siblings whose parents were the largest "anonymous" donors to our school.

176. After the principal's announcement that children who ordered lunch would now be required to bring their own reusable utensils from home in order to help the environment, had a child remark, "Our parents pay $20,000 a year to this school, so the least they could do is give us forks and have the teachers wash them."

177. Had a teacher wonder why she was severely reprimanded by the school administrator after she allowed two students to climb on the school roof to retrieve a ball? "It was only a flat, one-story roof," she said.

178. Had a student respond after you told him how much you enjoyed meeting his parents at conferences, "You just saw their 'be nice to teachers' faces. Believe me, that's not what they look like or act like at home"?

179. Had a parent report you to the principal after a conference because you told her that you were somewhat frustrated with her daughter Paige's continuing defiant behavior? "Good teachers," she told the principal, "should *never* be frustrated when working with children."

180. When learning about the American Revolution, had a group of fifth graders choose to learn, interpret, and sing the lyrics of two songs from the show *Hamilton?* When collaborating on *The Schuyler Sisters* song, Hayden asked what the lyrics, "I am a trust fund baby," mean. His group buddy, Jacob, offered an immediate and very serious clarification with the explanation: "You know how Jason brags that his parents and grandparents only drive Mercedes and Maseratis and that his dad and grandfather fly their own plane? Well, that makes him a trust fund baby." With no further reaction to this explanation, the group refocused and got right back to work.

181. Just after the legalization of marijuana in California, had a fourth grader share that her mom has al-

ways used marijuana when she makes roasted chicken. Knowing the student's mother very well, I called her during my break to let her know what her daughter said. The mother had trouble catching her breath from laughing so hard. "And you told me that Elizabeth is reading on grade level?" she responded. "You'd better recheck her reading level because the jar with the herb I use quite often is clearly labeled 'marjoram'."

182. At Welcome Back to School Night, handed out a detailed list of "Parent Excuses to Avoid During Conferences" beginning with: "Aww, he/she is just like me when I was his/her age"?

183. Told a mother and father of one of your students that they won the Parents of the Year Award? How refreshing it was to hear them begin an 'I'm Concerned About Your Child' meeting by declaring, "Okay, we don't care what anyone else did. Just tell us how we can help Danny be more responsible for his own actions."

184. Reluctantly accepted a student's response that it is not that important to learn to write her name in cursive because fingerprint identification and face recognition have already begun to make signing one's signature on documents obsolete?

185. Applauded your principal's perfect response to an unplanned series of events? After dividing the class into five groups of four, I challenged each group to find a way to drop an egg from the second floor balcony without it breaking. After completing the assignment, the groups cheered each other on as two of the first three

groups were successful. At the exact moment the fourth group dropped its layers of cotton and cellophane enveloped egg, the principal, Mr. David, unknowingly walked right under its descending path. As the egg made contact with the top of his bald head, the kids gasped. Without missing a beat, Mr. David grabbed the unbroken egg, looked it over carefully, and pointed to a large crow that was flying by. "Wow!" he exclaimed, pretending not to notice the now hysterical fourth graders on the balcony above him, "That mama bird sure knows how to lay an egg on target!"

186. While discussing a novel with your seventh-grade English class and feeling pleased that the students were attentive and focused, hear a marble-like, clinking sound on the floor? I was speechless when I realized that the glass eyeball of one of my students had fallen out of her eye socket and was bouncing around the room.

187. Had the pleasure of teaching a kindergartener with such a contagious and vivid imagination that all of the other kids in the class couldn't wait to play with her during free-time? I mentioned this to Janice, the child's mom, after school one day and also gave the example of how Eden loves to pretend that her real name is Sarah and that her mom's name is Linda. In fact, I told her that sometimes Eden even asks me and her friends to call her Linda during class. Janice's face visibly paled, and she pulled me aside to be sure no one overheard what she whispered to me: "I was wondering if you noticed Eden showing some strange behavior. She has been doing this since she was three years old. A few months ago, we had

her checked out by a psychic. We're convinced that Eden has memories of a past life." Who am I to disagree?

188. Witnessed a passionate kiss in the school parking lot between two of your students' parents who were married to other people?

189. Had a child bring extra clothes to school in case he vomited because he woke up feeling nauseous?

190. Had to assure the extremely devout, uptight mother of a very overprotected ninth-grade student that it was certainly age-appropriate for her son to know, as she put it, "the facts of life." You really had to constrain yourself from adding that her son could probably enlighten her.

191. Felt like asking the lovely, supportive, and cooperative parents of one of your most difficult students if there was a possibility that their son had been switched at birth?

192. Had a parent, accompanied by her very own search party of four, walk into your classroom before school began to look for her six-year-old daughter's lost tooth?

193. Had your class learn one of the most memorable lessons about the importance of American patriotism and the gift of being an American citizen by the parent of one of your students? When Mrs. Zaslavsky, a Russian immigrant and mother of one of my fourth-grade girls, asked if she could join the class when I taught the Amer-

ican election process in preparation for the 2016 presidential election, I agreed with pleasure. Mrs. Zaslavsky was studying for her American citizenship test and wanted the "privilege" of learning about the American government along with her daughter. What a role model she was for the entire class! She explained that the rights American citizens take for granted are not even known in Russia; the Bill of Rights, the systems of checks and balances, and the free, electoral process do not exist in the country she left. The kids were mesmerized by her passion and love for America. At the end of the unit, the children surprised Mrs. Zaslavsky with an honorary certificate of American citizenship that was signed by all of the students. And on Election Day, Mrs. Zaslavsky surprised the kids with ice cream and a red, white, and blue cake to thank them for their support and to proudly show them her Certificate of Naturalization.

194. Had a parent insist that her child must have cheated when he earned an outstanding grade on his social studies test?

195. Had a very shy, quiet, insecure, and seemingly afraid of her own shadow parent timidly ask you why her daughter is so shy, timid, insecure, and seemingly afraid of her own shadow?

196. Had to politely tell a parent who lived on the same street as you, that it was not okay to have her daughter knock on your door several times a week to ask for help with homework and school projects?

197. Had a very embarrassed parent email you that

instead of putting a snack bag of Cocoa Puffs in her daughter's lunchbox, she accidentally packed the bag of kibbles that were meant for her dog when he went to doggie day care?

198. Screamed at least a dozen expletives when you accidentally deleted 26 detailed comments when writing report cards?

199. Had to admonish two second-grade boys for bringing a jar of black pepper and bubble bath to school? It seems that they thought it would be fun to replicate the antics of George and Harold, two of the main characters in the popular *Captain Underpants* series, who, in one of the stories, sprinkle black pepper on the pom-poms of the cheerleaders and pour bubble bath in the school band's instruments. The kids were caught when they asked a very astute second-grade teacher where the school keeps its pom-poms and trombones.

200. Completely unannounced, without prior warning, and seemingly oblivious to the consequences of her actions, had a parent interrupt your class while the kids were taking a final to surprise her daughter with two very large mylar balloons in honor of her birthday?

201. Called your sister and jokingly tell her that you were tempted to call Child Protective Services on her for lack of proper child supervision? Your niece, who attended the same school at which you taught, told you that the juice in her thermos was really nasty and sour. The night before, my sister, Randi, and her husband hosted a family holiday dinner at which there were carafes

of wine for the adults and grape juice for the children. My sister quickly realized that the carafe of leftover red wine was accidentally refrigerated instead of the grape juice. It took only a little backtracking to realize that when making her own lunch, my 11-year-old niece had unknowingly poured the wine into her thermos.

202. Wondered if it was inappropriate or if you were just behind the times when there were three separate Amazon deliveries for three different students at your school from parents who wanted to be sure their children had the books, and in one case, a costume, they needed for a project?

203. After learning about homonyms, had a very eager child come to school the next day very anxious to share some "real" homonyms with the class? "Sure," I replied, pleased that the child had taken the lesson to heart. With that, he pulled out a plastic baggie, turned it inside out and said, "Watch some of the *fleas* that were on my dog *flee*." Well, not only did the *fleas flee*, but I also watched 21 other students flee out the door, as well.

204. Had the parent of a kindergartener become very defensive when you told her that you had to speak to her daughter Daniella several times about the importance of telling the truth? The mother doubted that her daughter even knew what a lie was because in the television show, *Law and Order*, the detectives said that young children are good witnesses because they don't know how to lie.

205. Had a child bring chocolate covered matzo to school to share with the class as she read a book about

the Jewish holiday of Passover and the significance of the different foods that are part of this holiday tradition? The next day, little Brady, one of Alisha's non-Jewish classmates, brought a box of Cheerios to school for the same Jewish holiday. Alisha quickly reminded him that anything made with oats should not be eaten during Passover. Brady became very upset and told Alisha that his mom said that she bought this in the "passed over" section of the supermarket for food that was on sale and they wanted to get rid of.

206. Asked a young child, who you were sure did not yet know how to tell time, why he was constantly turning around to look at the clock in the back of the room? Evidently, his parents had told him that each classroom clock had a hidden camera so that parents could check on the behavior of their children at any time.

207. Had a parent tell you that you will know when her son, Raffi, lies because he will close his eyes when he talks to you? Just as she believed as a little girl, her son is convinced that when children lie, teachers and parents have the magic power to see a little man dancing to the tune of *La Cucaracha (The Dancing Cockroach)* in their eyes.

A few weeks later, Raffi tightly shut his eyes and denied that he called one of his friends the "S" word (stupid). When he opened his eyes, I began to hum the *La Cucaracha* song. Raffi looked at me in shock and declared, "My mom's right! But I thought that the only magic powers that teachers have is that they can see what's going on behind them because they have eyes in the back of their heads!"

208. Wondered why a child was so often telling her classmates to "shut up and stop talking"? You had your answer at the first and very uncomfortable parent/teacher conference, when Bella's mother told Bella's father to "shut up and stop talking" every time he tried to say something.

209. Told the mother of a preschool child that you were concerned about her daughter's aggressive behavior: pushing, shoving, throwing chairs, temper tantrums, etc.? The mother's immediate response was that her daughter was much more intellectually advanced than her peers and that she was obviously frustrated when the other kids "didn't get it" as quickly as she did.

210. Actually felt relieved and even a bit like celebrating when you were sick with bronchitis and could not accompany your boisterous and often unruly class on a field trip?

211. Have you ever felt like sending a letter like the following to the parents of your students at the beginning of the school year?

Dear Parents,
Please know that I am a professional educator. I went to a university for over five years to earn my teaching credential. I spend hours writing lesson plans, developing strategies, keeping documentation, and attending, often on my own time and at my own cost, professional development courses to learn about the latest trends in education. I then use all of the above to guide instruction,

inspire passion, implement empathy, show compassion, teach manners, support the social structure and culture of our school and classrooms, stay informed about blood-borne pathogens, notice and monitor the health of kids, keep a diligent watch for possible school intruders, provide comfort and kind words, welcome visitors to our classrooms, provide help to beginning teachers, encourage the discouraged, rally-on the confident, differentiate the instruction, give alternative assessment when needed, collaborate, maintain good relationships with the faculty and community, refer for speech and testing, refer to O.T. screening, make phone calls to countless sources, organize field trips, write school improvement plans, implement those plans, spend countless hours outside the classroom, and, after all that, sometimes even have to defend myself to the very people who I am hell-bent on helping.

As the school year begins, know one thing for sure. I have your child's best interest at heart always and in all ways. I thank you in advance for your support.

Your child's teacher,

Ms. S.

We Couldn't Make This Stuff Up

"The Mafia Stole My Homework!"

"But it's true, Mrs. Shane. It's all true," the five-foot-tall, dark-haired woman cried in a heavy Russian accent as she frantically crossed herself over and over in the school parking lot. (Now that in itself was perplexing because Mrs. Sokolov and her family are Jewish.) "The Russian Mafia did take Olya's homework. It was awful, so awful," Mrs. Sokolov insisted as she continued to cross herself, tears streaming down her face.

The year was 2001, and, I, as a veteran teacher—and mother—had heard countless and very imaginative excuses about why homework assignments were not completed. But blaming the Russian Mafia!? It was all I could do to keep a straight face as I looked over the woman's head and saw the incredulous look of my principal, who had overheard everything.

It all started when Olya, a quiet, shy, but very capable fourth-grade student, was given a California Gold Rush research assignment three weeks earlier. Her assignment was to write about the ways in which gold was mined. Although ample time was given in class to complete a great majority of the research and write an outline, Olya, as well as several other students, fell a little behind and were given an extra week to complete their assignment at home. I thought that this was a generous extension, but being realistic, I was still keeping my fingers crossed that everyone would have their outlines in class on time so that I could proceed to the next step with all kids on board.

Even before the assignment was due, all of the kids had handed in his/her work. Everyone...except Olya.

The Monday morning the assignment was due, Olya was not even in school. I was really surprised at about 2:30, as we were working on our last assignment of the day, Olya arrived and walked reluctantly into the classroom. I didn't even have a chance to greet her before she burst out crying in front of the whole class and blurted out, "The Russian Mafia took my homework!"

Olya's classmates looked at her dumbfounded. They had no idea what the Russian Mafia was and stared at their classmate in silence. I looked at her dumbfounded, as well! "What! The Russian Mafia stole your homework!?"

I immediately asked my classroom aide to take over. With my arm around Olya's shoulders as she continued to cry, we walked to the school office so that I could receive much needed guidance from Principal Amanda Collier about how to handle this perplexing Russian Mafia situation. (I must admit that as I passed a few of my colleagues, I rolled my eyes and mouthed the words, "You won't believe this.")

Mrs. Collier kindly offered Olya—and me—a soothing cup of hot chocolate and invited her to sit between us and tell her story. Mrs. Collier and I tried our best not to gasp as the usually shy and submissive nine-year-old, who needed just a little prodding for details, enthusiastically and with much drama divulged her story. Although not verbatim, this is the essence of what Olya said:

"Oh, Mrs. Collier, I was at my aunt's house on Friday night with my cousins and I was doing my homework in the dining room. My mom and aunt were in the kitchen making food, and my dad and uncle were watching the television. They were sitting on the floor because my aunt and uncle just moved there and didn't have furni-

ture. Then, there was a lot of banging on the door that was real loud and then the door broke open. Everyone screamed and I ran to my mom with my cousins. My mom and aunt screamed more and started crying and so did me and my cousins. And then three men who were wearing really scary masks pointed guns at us and made us all stand against the wall. I was shaking so much. The men were yelling in Russian and threw big plastic bags at us and told us to put everything in it–even the food. They yelled at my mom and my aunt to take off their rings and grabbed them real hard. But later my mom said the diamond rings were fakes, so I guess that was good. Then one of the men hit my uncle in the face with his gun and yelled at him to give him the money and the jewelry. But my uncle yelled that he just moved into the house, but the man didn't believe him and told my cousins and me to go upstairs to the bedrooms. And, Mrs. Collier, I was going up the steps and holding my homework and my hands were shaking, and the man told me to put my homework in the plastic bag and even my pencils. He was so mad. And then he tore my homework up. One of the men took the bottle my dad had and got really mad when it spilled all over. And then the men tied us up with ropes but not too tight. I was so scared."

Incredulous, Amanda and I looked at each other not really knowing what to think. "Did you call the police?" I asked.

"Oh, no, Mrs. Wells," she answered sounding very upset. "My mom said we can't call the police or the Russian Mafia will come back and kill us. But then we got out and went home, and the next day we even went back and looked all over for my homework even if it was torn up, but it wasn't there."

"You went back to your aunt's house and looked for your homework, and it wasn't there?" I echoed.

"Yes," Olya responded nodding her head.

Thank goodness for the bell signaling that it was time for dismissal. I helped Olya with her jacket, took her hand, and, with Mrs. Collier close behind, walked to the parking lot where I knew Mrs. Sokolov was always one of the first parents waiting to pick up her child.

As calmly and as professionally as possible, I took Mrs. Sokolov aside and related everything her daughter had told me. To my astonishment, Mrs. Sokolov grabbed my hand and said, "But it's true, Mrs. Wells, it's all true."

"And you didn't call the police?" I responded.

"The Russian Mafia will kill us," she replied.

"The Russian Mafia will kill you," I repeated. "Well, what about your sister's family? How are they?" I inquired rather dubiously.

"They're not here anymore. They rent truck and leave house in the middle of the night, so Russian Mafia can't find them. I don't know where they go." With that, Mrs. Sokolov firmly took her daughter's hand and, with both of them in tears, walked to her car and drove away.

Later that evening, as Amanda and I commiserated over a bottle of wine, we agreed that although Olya may not have completed her assignment, she was certainly gifted with one of the most creative imaginations of any child we ever taught–most certainly with the help of her mother.

Laugh Out Loud

"Butterflies for Breakfast"

The year we had a new principal, I thought was also going to be my last year teaching. I wasn't planning on retiring for at least 10 more years, but it was what happened that year that could have ended my career.

The goal of our new leader, as she so aptly stated at our first staff meeting, was to enhance the reputation of our already excellent school with more interactive school programs. Okay, sounds good. But just what did she have in mind, and was *she* going to play an integral part in making this happen? As our principal explained further, in order to enhance strong teacher/parent teamwork, each teacher would be asked to "volunteer" to serve on a committee with parent volunteers. These programs were to take place all year long, starting with a Welcome Back to School Ice Cream Social and culminating with a year-end Talent Show. To give my principal due credit, she had come up with the names and dates for these programs—but that was to be her sole contribution to our new "won't it be fun" and "collaborative" project.

By the way, all meetings were to take place after school, which my colleagues and I *very* much "appreciated", since we all know that being at school all day and then working into the evenings for weeks at a time is something we all relish! Never mind the fact that many teachers had to arrange additional after school care for their own children.

I felt a little easier knowing that the teachers' roles for these programs would be limited to that of facilitator: parents would be responsible for spearheading all programs, and at least one parent per committee was an experienced program volunteer.

However, at our first meeting to plan the spring event for which I had "volunteered," the parent volunteers and I sat in a room just staring at each other. Not one parent was taking the lead. After too many moments of silence, I felt that I had to say something. "For those who don't already know, my name is Jan Cole, and I have the pleasure of teaching second grade. How about we go around the room and introduce ourselves." After this...silence once more. And so I began again. "Who would like to be the chair of this event?" I questioned hopefully. As I looked around, I felt like I was observing deer in headlights! In the interest of getting home before midnight, I offered to be the chairperson of the event. Their collective breaths could have filled a hot air balloon! (So much for parents taking the lead.)

After a few moments of thought, and assuming correctly that anything I proposed would be accepted, I suggested that our PTO purchase butterfly kits for each of our kindergartens through fifth-grade classrooms. It would be fun for the kids to watch the life cycle of a butterfly right before their very eyes. To make it even more educational, I suggested that the kids keep a journal with the pictures they drew and written observations of the metamorphosis. We—I mean, I—could then plan a culminating event where all of the classes would set their butterflies free at the same time. What a beautiful vision! As I looked around, a nod of heads in unison from this group of selective mutes indicated to me that we were all "in agreement" of "our" plan.

I, in my "supportive" role, took it from there. I asked the PTO to order the butterfly kits, informed my colleagues of "our" in-class objectives, and met with the school's in-house rabbi (we are a Jewish day school) to plan a meaningful ceremony for the release of these fragile and beautiful new lives.

Finally, the day came for this momentous event. It was a perfectly beautiful spring morning. The entire school gathered in excitement on the many steps leading to our school with their boxes of live butterflies. Everyone, students and teachers alike, felt very protective towards their charges; after all, they had all been an integral part of this amazing life cycle event.

Each class was seated according to grade level. Kindergarteners were given front row seats to watch their "babies" leave "the nest." Our principal, administrative assistants, P.E. teacher, guidance counselor, and school librarian stood proudly at the top of the steps. We were thrilled that even our local newspaper sent a reporter and photographer to capture this culminating event.

Rabbi Benjamin asked that we recite the *Shehecheyanu*, which is the blessing that Jewish people say to thank God for being able to celebrate a joyful occasion. We sang a few songs, contributing to an atmosphere that was absolutely spiritual! Then, in unison, we counted down: "10, 9, 8, 7, 6, 5, 4, 3, 2, 1...Freedom!!!!" As each teacher opened the door to a butterfly box, all of the children began to applaud and scream with glee as the lovely creatures gracefully ascended towards the sky. It was absolutely perfect...for a few glorious seconds. Suddenly, and without warning, a flock of hungry, humongous, horrifying black crows swooped down and devoured all of our beautiful butterflies. Screams of joy became shouts of horror. Many children were crying.

"Oh, my God!" I exclaimed in horror as I shut my eyes, realizing that I had traumatized the entire school body in one full swoop—no pun intended.

Somehow, Rabbi Benjamin was able to gain control of the entire school population by speaking loudly into the microphone about how we had all done a mitzvah—a good deed—by providing starving birds with a healthy breakfast. God bless Rabbi Benjamin! He quickly dismissed each class back to their rooms. I silently recited the *Kaddish*, the Jewish prayer for the dead.

I held my hands over my eyes and furtively looked through the cracks so that I could see the reactions on the face of each of the kids—and teachers—as they walked back to their classes. Not too bad, I surmised, as I let out a very long and deep breath that could have filled a hot air balloon.

When I got to the teachers' lounge at lunchtime, I entered to find a huge poster on the wall created by our computer teacher. On it was a photo of humongous horrifying black crows with the caption:

WANTED: DEAD OR ALIVE!

These Felons Have Eaten Our Dear Butterflies for Breakfast!

The names and email addresses of each of the parent planning committee members were listed in red as the contacts for anyone having information leading to the arrest of the crows.

Laugh Out Loud

"Grey vs. Gray"

It was January 2012, and the fifth-grade boys and girls had just been assigned a historical fiction book report. Our school library had a particularly well-stocked collection of this genre, so I was confident that all of the kids would be able to choose something that interested them. The librarian pointed the kids in the right direction, and, I must say, I was quite impressed with their enthusiasm. All was going great; within 15 minutes, most of the kids had chosen their books and, after showing them to me or the librarian for approval, were actually sitting at the round library tables sharing what they had chosen with their peers or reading. Just when I thought that we were almost ready to go back to class, there was an unexpected disruption. It seems that Alexa, the class drama queen, glanced at the book her friend Sofia was reading, and shrilly yelled as she grabbed it from her, "You can't read that!" Of course, everyone looked up as Alexa, with Sofia angrily trailing behind her, ran up to me and waved the confiscated book in front of my face. "Mrs. G.," Alexa shrieked, "I can't believe that this book is in the library! Last week, my mom nearly killed me when she realized I was listening to her book group talking about it."

"Why, what's so bad about it?" Sofia demanded as she tried to grab the book back.

"I know it has something to do with sex and that my mom hid the book from me. Your mom was there too, Sofia."

Now the rest of the class was demanding to know the title of the book.

As Alexa passed the book around, one kid shouted, "Yeah, my mom is reading that, too." A second child piped in, "My grandma, aunt, and mom read it." To tell the truth, it seemed like most of the moms in the class had not-so-secretly read the book or were in the process of reading it, as well.

So much for class control...but that was due to the fact that the librarian and I were laughing so hard that tears were running down our faces. Our laughter was contagious because the kids started laughing, too, but they had no idea what they were laughing at. Their laughter turned to stunned silence when I, still laughing, took the book and held it over my head for everyone to see. I collected myself long enough to inform the class that the book in question, *Shades of Gray* by Carolyn Reeder, which was about the experiences of a 12-year-old boy during the Civil War, was, indeed, an excellent choice for a historical fiction book.

At the end of the day, laughing still, I sent an email to all of the moms in the class telling them about our library experience and suggested that they keep their copies of *Fifty Shades of Grey* by E.L. James under lock and key.

Immediately upon arrival at school the next day, Danny, one of my most outgoing students, was very excited to share with me that right after reading my email and speaking to another mom in the class, his mom told his 17-year-old sister to start getting dinner ready because she had to go to the bookstore.

Later that day, I received an email from Danny's mom thanking me profusely for my email.

Laugh Out Loud

"The Rag"

Have you ever had so many bizarre incidents with a parent that even those that are the most bizarre seem absolutely plausible? Let me begin with the fact that I am very fortunate to teach in a diverse, multi-cultural school, one in which the students, parents, and staff alike truly enjoy a close, inclusive, and very supportive family-like environment.

And so it was with the lovely, sweet, kind, but very, very needy Mrs. B. and her two just as lovely, sweet, kind fifth-grade twin daughters. Nicole was in my class, and her identical twin Mariana was in my co-teacher's class. Mrs. B.'s daily laments about her daughters seemed to have no end. Mr. and Mrs. B. and their extended family had come to the United States when their girls were almost two years old. Of course, it was very important for Mr. and Mrs. B. to maintain much of their beautiful culture and customs while trying to assimilate into the melting pot of their new country. As a school, this was something we encouraged and loved. We looked for opportunities to share different customs and traditions with students and to connect the similarities of different cultures. However, Mrs. B. had a much more difficult time assimilating than her husband and most of her family. Everything seemed so overwhelming to Mrs. B., especially differences in child-rearing. But she was truly so sweet that the teachers and, especially Jill, our guidance counselor very patiently listened to and tried to accommodate her requests.

"Oh, please, Mrs. Jill," Mrs. B. would tearfully ask…

"Please talk to my girls about not fighting with each other."

"Please talk to my girls about not yelling at me."

"Please talk to my girls about not watching so much television."

"Please talk to my girls about reading more."

"Please talk to my girls about taking a bath every night."

"Please talk to my girls about washing their hair more."

"Please talk to my girls about doing their homework without arguing."

"Please talk to my girls about letting their grandmother teach them how to cook food from our culture."

"Please talk to my girls about not saying bad words."

After walking into the school office following a teachers' meeting, Mrs. B. saw Mrs. Jill conferring with a few teachers, including me. Mrs. B. frantically grabbed Mrs. Jill's hand, held it tightly between her own, and pleaded, "Oh, Mrs. Jill, please talk to my girls about the 'CURSE!'"

The CURSE? Now, this caught everyone's undivided attention! It was a few days before Halloween, and the first thought that came to my mind was that it had something to do with this trick-or-treat fun-filled holiday.

Ever the professional, Jill took Mrs. B. aside, told her that she had already scheduled meetings and classes for the rest of the day, and made an appointment to meet before school the next morning.

"But what if they men-stru-ate before then, Mrs. Jill?"

After a few tactful questions, Jill determined that it was not likely.

Throughout the years, my colleagues and I have been known to play fun and very creative pranks on one another; some were truly classic, as I hoped the one that was now formulating in my mind would be. I pride myself—just a little—on being able to imitate accents and disguise my voice. I hoped that it would work this time.

With the main characters—the staff and my fellow teachers—in full compliance, I immediately put my ploy into place. First, the principal's assistant, Anise, interrupted Jill at her not-so-important meeting and told her that she was needed in the office immediately. Anise told Jill that it seems that Mrs. B. was having a melt-down on the phone and, very politely, insisted on speaking with Jill immediately. In the meantime, the vice-principal, trying not to laugh, graciously invited me to use her office and get into character. She walked out, closed the door, and gave me a 'thumbs up' as she left to join Jill and our fellow conspirators. I only allowed two "witnesses" in the room with me who were sworn to silence. Then, I turned the swivel chair to face the wall so that I would not be distracted, took a deep breath, cleared my throat, covered the mouthpiece of the receiver with a scarf, and assumed my character—Mrs. B.—accent and all. As Jill hurried into the office, about four of my cohorts, as well as the vice-principal and Anise, assumed their choreographed positions and did a pretty good job of maintaining straight faces as the conversation began. Jill was handed the phone and the conversation began:

Jill: "Hi, Mrs. B. I understand you're upset and can't wait until we meet tomorrow. What's going on?"

(Jill was pantomiming, with true empathy, tears on her face to indicate that Mrs. B. was crying.)

Mrs. B (me): "Oh, Mrs. Jill," I pretended to cry in what I thought was a perfect Mrs. B. accent. "You know how much I love you. [Mrs. B. always prefaced conversations with Jill by telling her how much she loved her.]

I am very nervous about how to talk to my girls about men-stru-a-tion and the special customs we have in our culture to celebrate this time in a girl's life."

Jill: "Please don't worry, Mrs. B. In a few weeks I'll be leading the fifth-grade age-appropriate *'Sex Talk'* with the girls, and Mr. Samson will be with the boys. You signed the forms at the beginning of the school year. Remember?"

Mrs. B. (me): "Oh, yes, Mrs. Jill. I remember. Thank you. I love you so much. Thank you." (I stifled a fake sob). "Now can I ask you to do something special for Grandmother and me?"

Jill:"Sure, whatever I can do to help."

Mrs. B. (me): "Oh, thank you. Thank you so much. You see, we have a custom in my culture when a girl first men-stru-ates and becomes a 'woman.'

It is called the *On the Rag* ceremony."

Eye-witness accounts: Jill was now rolling her eyes and making the crazy sign with her finger. Oh, my God! she mouthed.

Jill "*On the Rag* ceremony?" Jill asked incredulously.

Mrs. B. (me): "Oh, yes. Mrs. Jill. It is a beautiful ceremony."

Jill: "Well, why don't you tell me more about it,"

Jill asked cautiously and mouthed,

Oh, my God! once again.

Mrs. B. (me): "Oh, yes, Mrs. Jill. When a girl in my country first men-stru-ates, the grandmother or mother gives her a beautiful white cloth for her to use on the first day. Then we take the rag—the cloth is called rag after it is stained—and carefully wrap it in a red silk bag. (Pause) "Mrs. Jill, are you still there?"

My eyes were tightly shut at this point, attempting to swallow my laughter. I dared not turn around to look at my friends.

Jill: "I am, but I don't understand how I can help you."

Jill was now grimacing and holding out her hands in mock surrender.

Mrs. B. (me): "Please listen, Mrs. Jill. It is such a beautiful ceremony.

Grandmother takes the silk bag and walks with her granddaughter and female family and friends to a garden to say a prayer of thanks, plant a new tree, and bury the red silk bag next to it."

My friends were now audibly stifling their laughter—even snorting.

The women in the office with Jill were, as well, but turning their heads so she couldn't see their faces.

Jill: "I'm sorry, Mrs. B., but I'm still not understand-ing."

Mrs. B. (me): "Oh, Mrs. Jill. I'm hoping that when Nicole and Mariana, have their first men-stru-a-tion, we can have a beautiful On-the-Rag ceremony with the girls in their classes. Just girls. No boys. Grandmother will come and we will walk to the beautiful school garden. I will donate a tree and we can bury the silk bag and celebrate with all the girls. Of course, we will be honored if you and the teachers come, too. I will prepare a delicious lunch with food from my culture and special sweets in red silk bags for dessert."

My chosen witnesses were laughing more loudly now, and I was trying to shush them by waving my arm at them from behind the chair.

Jill's witnesses also laughed as she ran her fingers through her hair.

Jill: "Mrs. B." Jill began slowly, choosing her words carefully, "I understand that this is a beautiful ceremony in your culture.

However, you're requesting something that I really can't help you with. I know that there are school rules that do not permit such a personal celebration. You know I've tried to be as supportive as possible throughout the years [huge sigh]. I'm sorry."

Mrs. B. (me): "Oh, but please try, Mrs. Jill. I love you. It is so important to me and Grandmother."

Jill:"Do the girls know about our conversation?"

Mrs. B.(me): "Oh, No!! First, they must learn about men-stru-ation.

Then, you must please help me to tell them about the

On the Rag ceremony. They will not want to do it if Grandmother or I ask them."

By this time, Jill really did have to go. She made a cut/stop action motion on her throat and, from all accounts, took another deep breath before continuing . . .

Jill: "I know you are very anxious about this, Mrs. B. I need to go now, but I promise we will continue our talk in person within the next week or two."

Mrs. B. (me): "Oh, thank you, Mrs. Jill. I love you."

As soon as Jill hung up the phone, our kind, caring, sensitive, loving guidance counselor burst out laughing harder than anyone had ever heard her laugh before. She was getting ready to share this "unbelievably believable" story with the others in the office—obviously, no children were present! I assumed a neutral expression, opened the door of the vice principal's office, and walked out.

"Oh, my God, Maxi!" Jill exclaimed when she saw me. Her eyes were bulging and her head was shaking back and forth. "Never in all of my years as a teacher or guidance counselor have I ever experienced what just happened." Trying to speak articulately between bursts of laughter, Jill began to tell us all about her incredible phone call.

At that point, I could contain myself no longer, and I literally fell on the floor in hysterics. Everyone in the office was laughing hysterically, as well. It took a minute or so for Jill to process what was going on around her.

"Okay, what's going on?" she asked slowly and suspiciously.

I stood up, looked at Jill, and, in my best Mrs. B.

imitation said:

"Oh, Mrs. Jill. I love you so much. It would mean so much to Grandmother and me if we can have an On the Rag men-stru-ation ceremony at school. I donate a tree."

If Jill's eyes were bulging before, they were almost coming out their sockets now.

"YOU'VE BEEN PUNK'D!" everyone cried in unison.

Jill looked from one friend's face to another, took a very deep breath, and, as good-naturedly as ever, burst into what seemed to be much relieved laughter. She then pointed a finger at me, and, in mock-anger, hissed: "But you sounded just like her! Just you wait. I'm gonna get you back good!"

I laughed, gave Jill a great big hug and said, "Can't wait!"

My Child Never Does Anything Wrong

"Anticipatory Response, Dreams, and Paper Bags"

Anticipatory Response Alert – "An increase in heart rate that typically occurs just before an activity is to be undertaken. It results from an increase in activity of the sympathetic nervous system causing the adrenal glands to release adrenaline and noradrenaline into the bloodstream."

- Oxford Reference

Ever since eight-year-old Spencer was in preschool, his teachers could count on one thing...an Anticipatory Response Alert every time he opened his mouth to speak. His teachers could count on this young man's prolific words of self-expression under any circumstances–provoked/non-provoked, stressful/non-stressful, fatigue induced/non-fatigue induced; happy mood/sad mood. No matter what behavioral interventions were used throughout the years, his disruptive behaviors didn't change. Fellow teachers, you get the picture. Top that off with the fact that every time we called Spencer's parents, they were extremely supportive...of Spencer, that is.

Everyone privileged to work with Spencer agreed that he was extremely intelligent but was gifted with the bare minimum of impulse control. Along with other observational behaviors with which my fellow colleagues are all too familiar, Spencer's teachers and guidance counselor had no doubt that Spencer had ADHD–Big Time. But, of course, we could not use that "label" until he was officially diagnosed. It was also all too apparent after three academic years of numerous parent/teacher interactions and both formal and informal meetings that, as the saying goes, "The apple (in this case the 'Spencer apple') doesn't fall far from the tree." I can't tell you how many times my colleagues and I kicked each other under the table at parent meetings, knowing full well that Mr. and Mrs. 'Spencer-Tree' were not focused on the issues, were very easily distracted, and their parting response would always be the same. His mom would indignantly and haughtily adjust her posture and plant the palms of her hands very firmly on top of the table. Then, in a very annoying, squeaky, high-pitched voice (similar to that of the sound a blown-up balloon makes when the air is slowly squeezed out of it) and, with a significant lisp, Mrs. Spencer-Tree would let everyone know that the meeting was adjourned by saying, "Spencer is just like his father. And, no, we will not have him tested because we don't want him labeled. He's a very sweet child, and we want to make sure he feels good about himself. We will talk with him at home, but the teachers must be more patient and understanding." (After many years, I can still imitate Mrs. Spencer-Tree verbatim.)

After the third parent/teacher meeting with the Spencer-Trees in four weeks, and with the full support of the guidance counselor and my wonderful principal, I told Spencer's parents that from now on, every time he exhibited unacceptable behavior that disrupted the class, I would have him go to the office and call them to report, in his own words, what he had done. After all, I was feeling very magnanimous and wanted to be sure that Spencer's parents were also able to fully enjoy all of their child's "Spencerisms." I actually don't think that

Spencer minded the routine. At least he was expending much-needed energy on his office-runs each time he checked-in with his parents.

About two weeks after our last parent/teacher meeting, and following Spencer's fourth mandatory march to the school office for disrespectful behavior in my class, Amy, the office manager, came running to my room during my prep time. Somewhat appalled, yet not able to suppress her nervous laughter, she proceeded to tell me what had just happened:

Upon entering the main school office, Spencer knew the routine. He confidently walked into the guidance counselor's office (which was adjacent to that of the office manager) and reluctantly greeted her with a nod. He picked up the receiver, plugged in his dad's office number—he was privy to the direct line—and, very matter-of-factly, told him the latest "Spencerism." (Of course, I had just emailed the guidance counselor, and she was expecting him.) *It took about five minutes for Spencer to clearly and, somewhat honestly, articulate to his dad how he had disrupted the class. For the first time, Spencer cried as his father reproached him very loudly for an equal amount of time. The guidance counselor then gently took the receiver from Spencer and spoke to the father for a few minutes. She then asked Spencer if he had anything else to say to his dad. Spencer slowly and tearfully nodded his head, took the receiver, and screamed in a voice that reverberated to the adjoining offices... "GO HAVE A WET DREAM!" With that, Spencer slammed the receiver down as hard as he could.*

Fast forward seven years later to high school. Valentine's Day! My dear friend, Carly, taught at the same school at which Spencer now attended. For years, we have regaled one another with student/parent stories—call it a form of self-help therapy—and she had certainly heard about Spencer. (Of course, when I spoke with Carly I changed his name to maintain confidentiality.) Cell phones now ruled, and as I got in my car at the end of the day, my phone rang. It was Carly. Without even a greeting, she blurted, "You won't believe this one." It seems that just as Carly was about to take attendance and begin her day, not one of her students responded to the morning bell. Instead, her 15-year-old tenth-grade students were in the back of the room animatedly gathered around the desk of one of the most "challenging" students. In fact, this student's desk was strategically placed in the back of the room so that if he felt the need to "express himself" he could walk out of the room to settle down without disturbing anyone else. This was great planning because the young man made good use of his accommodation at least three times before 9:00 a.m. almost every day.

Carly has a phenomenal sense of humor, which is a necessary asset when working with young teenagers. She knew that the kids were very excited about Valentine's Day, a day on which many of the kids traditionally revealed their not-so-secret crushes. So when Carly, with a ready smile on her face, joined her class in the back of the room to see what was going on, her expression changed from one of fun anticipation to that of a horrified *Oh my God, how am I going to handle this!* (as in "discipline"–not literally). It seems that instead of sharing the usual red and white cards and cheap sweets in recognition of this special day, the students were reacting to the Valentine's Day "share" that the most "challenging" student had placed on his desk on top of a very crumpled brown paper bag with a red heart sticker. Carly was confident that most of the kids had no idea what they were looking at; in fact, at first, Carly wasn't even quite sure herself that what she was looking at was, indeed, what she thought it was. As Carly's processing hiccup cleared, she realized that some of the kids were laughing hysterically, others laughed nervously, a few kids muttered, "Ew, disgusting." And another, very wise young man said to the boy seated at the desk, "You're an idiot. You're really going to get in trouble!"

"Get in trouble, is right!" Carly sputtered as the kids parted so that she could get right next to the desk on which the forbidden item sat. Quickly putting the "object" back in its crumpled brown paper bag with the red heart sticker, Carly just glared at her student, and he automatically followed her on an all too familiar walk to the principal's office. A 9-1-1 meeting by the guidance counselor and the school's powers-that-be was called. The boy's parents were called and told that they needed to meet with the principal immediately to discuss the contents of the very crumpled brown paper bag with the red heart sticker that their son had brought to school.

The atmosphere was definitely professional yet strained as the parents took their seats. Upon seeing the very crumpled paper bag with the red heart sticker and its contents, the mother's response, in her very annoying squeaky, high-pitched voice (similar to that of the sound a blown-up balloon makes when the air is slowly squeezed out) and, with a significant lisp was an astounding: *"He asked me to buy it as a joke. I told him he might get caught...(sigh) He's just like his father."*

I'm not going to go into more details about the disciplinary measures that were taken. However, many years later, rumor has it that on the day the guidance counselor retired, the last thing she added to her box of 35 years of cherished mementos was a very crumpled paper bag with a red heart sticker as well as its contents. The only thing that the new guidance counselor found in the desk drawer the first day of the new school year was an empty package of Energizer AAA batteries.

Administrators From Hell

I was inspired to share this story when, at the end of 2017, so many brave women began to find the courage to identify and speak out against some of the most well-known salacious powers-that-be in Hollywood and politics for sexual harassment and rape. Although not necessarily sexual in nature, psychological and emotional harassment and abuse of power also exist in workplace environments, and so many "underlings" are fearful of the consequences if they reveal the truth about how they are being treated.

With these revelations, I am especially proud of the fact that in 2012, with little support from my fearful colleagues, I did have the self-confidence and strength to publicly defend myself against the bully who just happened to be the principal of my school, and I came out on top.

My challenge to others:

Speak up. Stand up to bullies in the workplace.

Remember, the Emperor really isn't wearing any clothes.

Empowerment

"You, sir, are a demeaning, delusional, repulsive, repugnant, compulsive liar and a bombastic manipulative bully who, for the past, almost three years, has single-handedly changed the warm and loving collaborative atmosphere of our school to one that is toxic and filled with anxiety and fear. Your responses and personal interactions have stifled the spontaneity and creativity of our wonderful staff, and I am not willing to put up with this anymore!"

There! I said it! I had no regrets. And I felt wonderful! Thousands of pent-up and suppressed brain bubbles that had been festering for over two years popped with the ferocity of a thunderstorm!

Upon my arrival to his office three minutes earlier, the object of my frustration, or as I like to call it, "fruckstration," was seated in his "Welcome to My Office" customary position: he was leaning back in his oh-so-comfortable padded leather office chair, arms behind his head with fingers interlocked, and a ubiquitous smug smile plastered on his face. To this day, five years later, I can still clearly picture his reaction to my diatribe with a satisfaction that has not diminished throughout the years. The back of his chair creaked as it moved in position to support his now straight-as-a soldier position, his hands fell to his lap, and his ubiquitous smug smile was replaced with an expression of shock and awe.

"He" and "his" obviously refer to the principal of my school, Robert Adams, a harbinger of the negative energy that had been breaching the confidence and emotional well-being of the entire staff for the past two years.

What was incredulous to me and most of my colleagues was that so many of us had been on the committee that had unanimously decided that Robert was our number one choice to try to fill the shoes of our much loved and respected retiring principal; after all, he was well educated, experienced, sociable, charismatic and apparently very self-motivated. He was very matter-of-fact and articulate about the positive changes he wanted to bring to our Coatesville, PA school, and his enthusiasm was contagious. What my fellow committee members and I did not know at the time of the interviews, but would painfully come to realize within the first year of his employment, was that Robert was also a brilliant manipulator, an insecure control freak, and a compulsive liar.

The first month of the new school year was actually quite pleasant and uneventful. By the fifth week of the new school year, however, indications that all was not as it seemed, became quite apparent. It all began with teacher observations. The great majority of the teachers were seasoned, experienced, confident educators. Our younger teachers were passionate about what they did, and we continued to learn from each other. Classroom visitations by Mike, our previous administrator, were welcomed. He would just pop in the classrooms several times a week with a warm smile and a helping hand, therefore getting a true perspective of the teaching that was going on. As chairperson of the language arts department and long-time mentor for student teachers, I was used to and welcomed the mandatory "formal" observations, as well, which were always no more intimidating than the weekly, informal visits by the principal. Each teacher also met with Mike monthly, or, as needed, to discuss issues at hand—there are always issues—and observation feedback that was supportive and helpful. Quite often, the teachers and staff found unexpected notes of support and appreciation in their mailboxes.

The first indication that things were going to be drastically different was when I noticed that two of the younger teachers, Lisa and Paige, were very upset and were comforting each other during the recess break. My maternal instincts kicked in, and when I asked them what was going on, each of their responses was the same. They said that the day before, Robert had been in each of their rooms to observe them for what he said was an informal first observation of the year. They each had a weird, uncomfortable feeling when, toting a large tan briefcase, he walked into their room with a serious expression on his face, greeted them with a nod of his head, sat on a chair in the back of the room, took out a large manila folder that held various forms, and, as he looked around the room and at the students, made numerous checkmarks on several of the forms. After 20 minutes, he made a few cursory remarks to a few of the kids and asked others some questions. Before he left Lisa's room, he walked to her desk, looked through her lesson plan book, and took cell phone pictures. Paige said that when he did not see the lesson plan book on her desk, he actually disturbed a pile of papers that she had put aside to be graded in an attempt to find it. Following his classroom visits, he emailed Lisa and Paige, requesting them to meet with him for separate twenty minute "debriefings" during their planning times the next day. His evaluation consisted of a review of the scores he gave each of them on the itemized checklist, at the bottom of which he had actually figured out their average scores. Neither of the young women knew how to react. He told Lisa that the time frame she had planned for math the day before was three—yes, three—minutes too long and that it interfered with the reading lesson time frame. He chided Paige for not having her lesson plan book in plain view. There was nothing positive about any of his remarks. They each said that they were totally confused and didn't know what to think when he dismissed them with an effusive smile, a handshake, and even called out to Paige so that all in the outside office could hear, "Thank you so much, Paige. Have a great day!"

Within the next three months, every teacher on the staff, except me, had the same type of observation and "debriefing". He would even pit teacher against teacher by shaking his head during "debriefings," and, with an obnoxious smug smile on his face, offer his critique with the same three words every time, **"Well, you know** (teacher's name), why don't you speak to (another teacher) and have her help you with (teaching goal). I'll send her an email and let her know to expect you. Mmmm hmmm." (He always concluded with a "Mmmm hmmm" in various decibel levels.) Peer coaching, readily assisting one another, and sharing new ideas and strategies with our family of teachers was what we always did.

Robert had a negative comment about almost every lesson he observed, with a minimum of positive feedback strewn in here and there. The positive energy of our school environment plummeted, and teachers felt intimidated and certainly less motivated to be more innovative in class–everything they did seemed to be negated. My friends knew that they and their peers were good, strong, and motivating educators and they were totally confused by Robert's responses. To make matters even more confusing, every time Robert interacted with teachers outside of the classroom, he greeted them almost gushingly in his high, falsetto-like sing-song voice as if they were the best of friends. What did everyone do? Nothing...except to anxiously complain to one another and perhaps take an extra Prozac each morning and imbibe a second glass of wine at night.

When it was my turn to be observed, I knew exactly what to expect when Robert walked in. To me, his actions seemed almost marionette-like as he took his seat in the back of the room, set down his briefcase, took out his notepad with the ubiquitous checklist, and began to check, check, check for about 20 minutes. He then, as expected, walked to my desk and took pictures of my lesson plans. I turned around, sighed, and rolled my eyes knowingly.

When I came to his office for my "debriefing" at 7:30 the next morning,

Robert was nowhere to be found. The office manager was not surprised, saying that Robert often didn't show up until close to 8:30, always with a seemingly plausible reason that was beginning to wear thin. Robert and I wound up meeting during my lunch break the next day. He was in his customary "meet with the principal" position. He opened my folder, took out his checklists, shook his head back and forth, "tsk-tsked" in seeming disapproval, grimaced and began, **"Well, you know, Hildy..."**

The first thing he had a problem with was the fact that I spent 22 minutes teaching math that overlapped by four minutes with what should have been my reading group time. (At least he was staying on script.) He then told me to reach out to my co-teacher, Carol, about how I could better balance my lesson planning. "Strange," I thought, "he asked Carol to reach out to me two weeks ago for the same purpose." He was now going over point by point—check by check—what he thought needed improving. But when Robert showed me two bright red tally marks that indicated that a child sighed two times, a green tally mark that indicated that one boy was not at all focused, and three blue tally marks to note that several kids were talking during my lesson, I stared at him in disbelief. Another **"Well, you know, Hildy..."** followed by "recent studies show that these are the behaviors that indicate that children are not being challenged." I continued to stare at him in disbelief as I processed what I was seeing and hearing. "Hold on, Robert," I challenged. "What recent studies? Show me! Children sigh, children talk during class, and there are many reasons why some children lose focus. In fact, I often notice that you do, as well, during staff presentations. (I couldn't help that dig.) So clarify what you are talking about." One more **"Well, you know, Hildy..."** Robert then began to double-talk in a way that made me begin to doubt myself; by the end of the school year, however, his manipulative double-talk and subtle and not-so-subtle lies became his undoing.

Did some of the teachers and staff members complain to Robert's superior? Absolutely! However, other than a few "I'll look into this," nothing satisfactory was done. Not only that, but Robert was sure to let the teachers know that he and Mr. Arnold, the headmaster, were "like this" and crossed his fingers to emphasize their connection.

I was one of the confident few who dared to challenge Robert's opinions and his many edicts, the purpose of which no one really understood. I also regularly asked him to rephrase and clarify what he said so that I could better comprehend his double-talk. How amazingly coincidental that Robert's "observations" in my class and subsequent ridiculous and confusing evaluations became more and more frequent. I respectfully— although sometimes more adamantly than others—called him on everything with which I disagreed, and he didn't like it one bit.

By the end of the year, the school atmosphere could definitely be characterized as toxic. But many of the "underlings" (that's how we were made to feel) didn't pursue their complaints further because they were afraid of losing their jobs in what was a very competitive market. We were also falsely convinced that Robert and Mr. Arnold were, indeed, "like this"–fingers crossed. Sound familiar, fellow teachers?

And so continued the noxious school atmosphere and deteriorating teachers' spirits throughout the second year of Robert's tenure as principal.

However, what was changing was that parents were beginning to understand that what they had first thought to be very friendly, social, and charismatic behavior by our new leader was now revealing itself to be obsequious and just sucking up to those with deep pockets.

The first day of Robert's third year as principal began with the usual staff and grade level meetings. Robert made his rounds to each grade level group, and, when he got to mine and listened to our ideas, his first response, with a shake of his head and a smirk on his face was … **"Well, you know, Hildy..."** Hmmmm! Welcome to year three!

The first few months were filled with an air of seemingly tangible tension as Robert continued his *modus operandi* from the two previous years. This year, however, teachers and staff members caught him in more manipulative lies—some seemingly benign at the time—and even more attempts to be flagrantly ingratiating to parents. If there was an issue between parents and teachers, Robert *always* took the side of the parents and, even in front of them, often demeaned the teachers with his, **"Well, you know, (teacher's name),** followed by "why don't you think about … " It got to the point that teachers were truly allergic to Robert and tried to avoid him as much as possible lest they have an explosive reaction. More than once, the vice-principal left for the day in tears over a "Robert" issue. The guidance counselor said that she was certain Robert had a major processing issue because of his responses and follow-ups in her interactions with him. Some teachers—especially me—did speak to Mr. Arnold. In fact, there were three meetings with the headmaster that I requested Robert to attend. At each meeting, he managed to twist whatever I said into something completely different than my point-of-view.

As a result of my meetings, as well as those of a few other teachers' meetings with Mr. Arnold, some of Robert's minor degrading behaviors were put on hold–temporarily. However, the professional, formerly joyful and supportive campus environment that existed before Robert took over as principal continued to deteriorate.

"S** t hit the fan" the first week of March, the week of parent/teacher conferences. My good friend, the vice-principal, called me at home to let me know that Robert was planning to call me into his office the next day to discuss a disturbing complaint about me made by the parents of one of my students. I had no idea to what she was referring because all of my conferences so far were very positive.

I was seething but, at the same time, was both mentally and emotionally prepared for a potential confrontation when I walked into Robert's office the next day during my 2:15 planning time, as per his expected summons. Slowly shaking his head and with a "tsk-tsk" of his tongue, he proceeded to tell me that Mr. and Mrs. Schreiber were extremely upset after meeting with me to discuss the academic progress of their daughter, Monica. Apparently, I told the couple, "in an extremely demeaning manner," that I was very upset and disappointed with Monica's lack of motivation and willingness to accept responsibility in completing assignments and preparing for tests. I stared at him in disbelief and totally refuted what he just said. In fact, the parents were the ones who were even more upset with their daughter's progress than I. To paraphrase Robert's response: **"Well, you know, Hildy,** this is what Mr. and Mrs. Schreiber reported, and they specifically asked that you don't talk to them about this and that I handle the situation administratively." Once again, I stared at him but, at this point, could not contain my anger. "You, Robert, are a (expletive) liar." With that, I walked out of his office. It seems that my expletives were loud enough to be heard in the adjacent office because when I stomped out, the administrative assistant gave me a two thumbs-up.

Defying Robert's admonitions, I walked to the dismissal area where Mrs. Schreiber was waiting for her daughter. She greeted me with a hug and thanked me for our very productive conference. I had no hesitation in repeating what Robert had just told me. Her response..."He's a (same expletive as mine) liar. I've had enough." She said that now that she thought of it, Robert had gone out of his way to ask them how our meeting went. She and her husband told him how upset they were with Monica and that we were working together to put a plan in place. With that, she literally mumbled to herself as she called her husband and asked that he come to the school right away because she was going to demand an immediate meeting with the head administrator, Mr. Arnold. She grabbed my arm and literally pulled me with her to his office. When Mr. Schreiber arrived fifteen minutes later, I walked behind the couple as they stormed into the head honcho's office. Mrs. Schreiber was in tears. It seems that this was not the first time she and her husband had met with Mr. Arnold to discuss concerns about the principal. In fact, their concerns, as well as those of other parents about his lying, she confided, have been ongoing since shortly after Robert first arrived. We left 30 minutes later, with a promise from Mr. Arnold to resolve the situation.

The next day I received an email from Mr. Arnold asking me to write, from my point-of-view, of course, a detailed report about what has been going on since Robert's employment. My report turned into the equivalent of a ten-page legal brief. When I shared the "brief" with my fellow-colleagues, they were all supportive and agreed with what I wrote; however, only two of them consented to put their signatures next to mine. Fear of retribution!

After first giving a copy of the "brief" to HR at the end of the day, I met with Mr. Arnold and waited while he read what I had written. His response was serious and decisive: "I promise that I will seriously look into the situation, and, if confirmed, take appropriate actions. Are you willing to share this letter with Robert at a meeting in which we are all present?"

"You bet I am," I replied.

At the meeting the next day, Robert was uncharacteristically speechless after he read my letter. And I felt so empowered!

However, I felt that I needed even more closure. So, the next day, I walked into Robert's office and, with the ferocity of a thunderstorm, verbally "popped" the seemingly thousands of pent-up and suppressed brain bubbles that had been festering in my head for almost three years. Once again, Robert was uncharacteristically mute following my diatribe, and I walked out of his office feeling proud, strong, confident, and so very much relieved.

At our last staff meeting of the year, Robert shocked many of the attendees by tearfully apologizing for anything he may have done to offend staff members in the past three years. Silent cheers of validation were "telepathized" from one staff member to another. He then announced that he had accepted another position as principal of a school in Massachusetts so that his daughters would have the benefit of living closer to their grandparents. (Yeah! Sure!)

The last day of the school year I must admit that I enjoyed a bit of juvenile glee when Robert, with his tan briefcase in hand, tripped and fell on the curb in the parking lot on his way to his car; one of the most satisfying images I have is of Robert frantically trying to recover and stuff the checklists contents of his briefcase back where they belonged.

A Child as the Teacher

I was fortunate to be able to teach at a very small private school. Most classes had less than 15 students—one class per grade level. I had an instructional aide, and the parents, for the most part, were very cooperative.

From the first day of school, Jack, a very precocious first grader, constantly challenged my authority. When he was asked to read from his reader, he often replied, "I don't feel like it." When I left my desk to read with another reading group, he promptly took my seat and called out, "Class dismissed!" When trying to teach the concept of the number zero, I asked the class, "Who in the room has purple hair?" Guess who raised his hand? Now guess who then had to take 15 minutes of class time to get control of 14 kids who were laughing hysterically. I was constantly having to do crowd control because of Jack's behavior.

After three weeks of frustration, I reached my limit with Jack when he screamed out during quiet reading time, "Shelly, I'm going out to the bathroom!" This child even had the nerve to use my first name! Finally, I had to ask myself: "How long does it have to take before I call this kid's father to come in for a conference? Why was I holding off arranging to meet with THIS PARENT when I would surely have met with any of the others under similar circumstances?"

There was no other choice. I had to call the father of this disruptive boy IMMEDIATELY. Fortunately, I knew this parent's work phone number *by heart* because he happened to be my husband.

"Hello, Stan? Sorry to bother you at work, but *your* son, Jack, has been very disrespectful to me since the first day of school. You need to leave work and come to school right now for a conference with me and *your* son.

"Shelly, Jack is OUR son. Can't we have this discussion at home tonight?"

"No!" I screamed almost hysterically. "I need for you to come to school NOW! I'm losing control of myself and of the other kids in the class, thanks to YOUR, okay, OUR son!"

"I'm on my way," Stan said while letting out a very deep and audible sigh.

I asked my aide to cover me so that I could take Jack to meet with his father in the conference room. I'll never forget how little Jack looked sitting in the huge chair at the long table, his dangling feet not even close to reaching the floor.

"Jack, do you have any idea why Mrs. Stanton asked me to leave my work to come to school today?" Stan asked in a very stern voice. I loved that Stan was calling me by my professional name–a respect not shown to me by *our* son.

Immediately, Jack began to cry. The mommy in me actually felt sorry for him for a moment.

"It's too hard having Mommy as a teacher," Jack whimpered. "She's always so busy with the other kids. She doesn't have time for me." I now actually felt *very* sorry for him. I realized how hard it must be for a six-year-old to have to share his mom day-in and day-out, five days a week, with 14 other kids.

I embraced Jack, promising to be more attentive to him in the classroom. "Always know you are my very special student. I am depending on you to help me do my job. I need you to set the example for all of the other kids. If you don't listen to me, no one else will. I love you more than anyone else, and I always will."

Hearing this, Stan pretended to whimper, "Can I please leave, Mrs. Stanton? I have to go to the bathroom!"

Sing, Sing a Song

Raise your hands if you can identify with this statement: Parents can often be more difficult to handle than their kids. Is it unanimous? Hmmm! Imagine that!

It was my first year of teaching, and I was about to begin my career as a starry-eyed novice. I was so excited to be assigned a third-grade class and eagerly looked forward to the first day of the school year to begin.

At our first staff meeting, about a week before the first day of school, my fellow teachers and I were given our class lists. A few of the second-grade teachers, whom I had met only a few days before, looked over my shoulder to see which of their last year's kids were in my room. Little did I know they were actually looking to see which of the third-grade teachers would be the grand prize winner! Who would have the "honor" of inheriting Mrs. X and her "genius" eight-year-old son for the new school year?

In unison, my colleagues sang out the names on my list: "Amy–hard worker and very focused; Brett–very supportive parents; Joshua–great kid; Kayla–sweetest girl ever; Michael G.–great attitude; Michael L.–you'll love him; Oliver…OLIVER!" Collective GASP! And then…commiserative laughter! Laura, who would soon become my very close friend, sighed as she handed me a blue straw–a very short one.

I looked up at my co-workers, and they looked down at me as they shook their heads with sympathetic smirks on their faces and burst into laughter again. I begged them to pull themselves together so they could give me the low-down on Mrs. X and, *gasp*–I mean Oliver. It seems as though Mrs. X had labeled her child

"gifted" from the time he entered our school in kindergarten. Unfortunately, no one on our staff agreed with
her assessment.

Each year, before the school year began, Mrs. X
would request a meeting with Oliver's teachers to in-
quire—actually demand—how his teachers would challenge her brilliant son. Throughout the years, teachers
avoided Mrs. X as much as possible (can you blame
them?) because even casual encounters with her resulted
in an interrogation of how Oliver was being challenged.

I started to sweat. I had not yet had the pleasure of
participating in a parent-teacher conference, and I was
not looking forward to starting off the year with one.

Thinking I was home free because I had not yet received a phone call from Mrs. X, I looked forward to
the first day of school with my students. As I opened
the door of my classroom to greet the children, I saw a
woman and her young son. Mrs. X had come to introduce herself. Evidently, the X family had just come back
from a trip, which was why she and her husband had not
attended the "get-to-know-you" parent/teacher meeting
the previous week. She asked if we could meet in my
room after school. "That would be great," I lied with a
forced smile.

Our first day of school was busy, passing out books,
going over class rules, etc. You know what it's like.
Before we knew it, it was time for morning recess. It
seemed that during the 15 minutes recess break, Oliver
chose to sing, in his very best voice, his original composition of *"I Love My Penis"* to any child within hearing
distance. The kids were horrified—although some were
laughing—and couldn't wait to tell on him as soon as
they got back to the room. *What was I to do?*

Luckily, at that moment, the assistant principal walked by my room. With eyes that were bugging out of my head and a frown on my face, I motioned for her to come inside my classroom. "Will you please watch my students so that Oliver and I can make a call to his mom?" Looking at me with a knowing and commiserative expression, she graciously accepted my request. I have no doubt that Oliver knew what I was going to share with his mother as he walked with his shoulders hunched and at a slow, shuffling pace to the office with me.

We went into the assistant principal's office, and I picked up the phone. I told Oliver to push the buttons of his home phone number. Mrs. X, having recognized the school's number, answered the phone with trepidation. I immediately assured her that Oliver was fine; he just had a song he wanted to sing for her. I handed him the receiver, but for some reason, he was reluctant to take it. Like any good teacher, I encouraged him to express his creativity to his mother. Oliver, with tears in his eyes, proceeded to sing, not as joyfully as before, of course, a very muffled version of *"I Love My Penis."*

When he finished, I took the phone from his shaking hand and asked his mom if she would still like to meet with me after school. Evidently, something must have just come up (no pun intended) for she abruptly told me that she could not make our pre-arranged meeting. It was not until the first scheduled parent/teacher conference, months later, that we finally met to discuss her very creative and gifted child.

The Sting

When I was the assistant principal at a middle school in Chicago, I was shocked when the cafeteria manager came to me and said that one of the cart ladies–the ladies who sold mini pizzas, chips, and snacks–thought that two of our up-until-now model students were giving her fake twenty-dollar bills. After they bought one and two-dollar items, they were given the change.

I met with the cart lady and devised a signal. She was to pull at her ear when the "suspects" approached with their twenty-dollar bills. Sure enough, at lunch duty that day, she pulled at her ear as the two boys stopped at her cart to make their purchases. I immediately approached the culprits and nabbed them! As we walked to my office to call the school police, the boys were in tears as they blubbered excuses for their actions.

"Hi, Officer, this is Beatriz," I started out, looking directly at the boys, "I have two young men in my office who have admitted to making counterfeit twenty-dollar bills on their home printer."

"Oh!" said a shocked Officer Fernandez, "That's a federal crime. You're going to have to call the FBI."

I immediately called the local FBI office, informed them what had happened and was told that agents would soon be on their way to the school.

Meanwhile, the boys' parents, who were model members of the community, rushed to the school as soon as they were called. Both sets of parents, who were obviously close family friends, lamented their shock as they all vouched not only for their own child's thus far untarnished character and reputation, but for that of each other's son, as well. It was true that both boys had very good academic records and were well liked by other students and their teachers. The boys sat in their chairs across from my desk as they continued to blubber their seemingly sincere apologies.

About an hour later, two 6'4" men in dark suits arrived. "Do you want these eighth graders arrested?" they asked me in front of all present. The parents were now petrified that their sons would go to the federal penitentiary, and their sons were just as terrified.

The agents and I met privately to discuss how best to handle the situation. After much discussion, we decided to have a "scared straight" meeting with the boys and their parents. During a very serious interrogation, the boys volunteered within seconds that on a whim and purely for fun, they Googled information about how to make counterfeit money. Obviously not thinking of the consequences, they used an inkjet printer and brought the printed bills to school purely as a joke. The boys were literally now shaking with fear. Never did they even consider that their prank might escalate to the point that they would get in such trouble, let alone the fact that the FBI and Treasury Agency might have to launch an investigation. Apparently, the "counterfeiters" even planned to reveal their prank and give back all the money. After about 30 minutes, it was obvious to all that these were essentially good kids who had made an extremely thoughtless and dumb choice.

To the relief of the embarrassed and now very angry parents, the FBI agents told the boys that they would be released to the custody of their moms and dads. Of course, they had to return all of the change that they had pocketed and give their word that they would earn money by doing chores to pay back the cost of the snacks they had "purchased."

One observant cart lady…two impulsive boys… four dumbfounded parents…life lesson learned.

Author Bio

Cheryl Kolker and **Jan Landau** had the pleasure of teaching at the same school for 25 years. They looked forward to writing this book for over 20 of those years, but as teachers in excellent standing and wanting to keep their jobs, dared not do so before they retired.

To Our Readers

Do you have your own unbelievably believable teacher quips/stories that you would like to see published? If so, please email them, along with you first and last name to <u>teacherquips2018@gmail.com</u>. We hope to publish a second edition of our book in the near future. If your quip/story is selected, we will send you a confirmation and list your name as a contributor to our book.

CPSIA information can be obtained
at www.ICGtesting.com
Printed in the USA
FSHW021843271019
63446FS